NADYA PRIMAK

Foot in the Door

My Self-Taught Journey to Becoming a Software Engineer

Copyright © 2019 by Nadya Primak

All rights reserved. No part of this publication may be reproduced, stored or transmitted in any form or by any means, electronic, mechanical, photocopying, recording, scanning, or otherwise without written permission from the publisher. It is illegal to copy this book, post it to a website, or distribute it by any other means without permission.

Second edition

This book was professionally typeset on Reedsy. Find out more at reedsy.com

Contents

Foreword		iv
1	Learning How to Learn	1
2	Programming Classes	8
3	The Ranks of the Employed	15
4	Early Mentors	23
5	Teaching Myself	29
6	Teaching Others	39
7	Transition Anxiety	45
8	LaunchCode	52
9	The Would-Be Hackathon	58
10	The Job Offer	66
Author Note		73
About the Author		75

Foreword

The tech industry never seems to stop growing. Each year more and more people are entering the field hoping it will revitalize their career or bring them the income to fulfill their dreams. I came to America as a four year old girl with immigrant parents who had this dream for me, and feared I might not choose a practical career because of the way they saw many American parents and teachers telling their kids they could accomplish anything simply by wishing for it hard enough.

Well, perhaps it was because of their pressure, or perhaps I was just always a practical person, but now at 28 years old I am a Mid Level Software Engineer with plenty of experience under my belt and a six figure salary. Although I have been a pretty practical person throughout my life, I have always tried to avoid being a selfish person. I have no interest in gloating about my accomplishments from a high horse. Instead I hope to share what I have learned with you, dear reader. Because I think with determination and hard work this is something you can also attain.

I have learned a lot since my college years where I took a few classes in computer science thinking it might be "useful" to have some technical know-how. I have moved four times, interviewed at dozens of jobs from startups to fortune 500 companies, and experienced what working in tech is like both from junior and senior positions at 6 different organizations.

It has been a wild ride, to say the least. Though you can expect your ride to be equally wild, and not everything that I experienced will necessarily apply, my hope is that what you read here will make your challenges a little easier, and the results a little sweeter.

Everyone dreams of having enough wealth to do whatever they want but like all things worth having in life, it takes work to get there. For those of you who have at least a little passion for tech, the perseverance to overcome bumps in the road, and the willingness to learn, this dream is truly within your reach. A quote I often hear around the developer community is that we are "expert Googlers." You don't have to know everything to get a good job in tech, but you do have to adopt a certain mindset that there will always be more to learn (just look up how many Javascript frameworks there are, for instance) and be excited rather than dismayed about that.

This book is divided into chapters where each chapter has two sections. Memories, where I talk about what I remember from that period in my life, and takeaways, where I discuss what I learned looking back. If you want to skip the storytelling and go straight to the advice, feel free to skip the memories section entirely. You might lose some of the context but you'll get the meat of what I'm trying to say. Ultimately there is no right or wrong way to read this book, but it was written in sequential order so it will make the most sense if you read it from beginning to end.

One last thing before we get to the good stuff. **If you enjoyed this book, I would super appreciate it if you took the time to leave a review.** Even a sentence or two makes all the difference. You can follow this link to leave a review.

1

Learning How to Learn

Memories

My start in tech happened well before I actually had the title of "Engineer" or "Developer". It started in a small town known primarily for being home to one of the most liberal (and most hipster) colleges in the country. I had mixed feelings about attending school there and was pressured in part by my parents to apply to schools in Ohio (they were moving there at the time).

Moving to Ohio meant leaving behind my friends and boyfriend (at the time) in Minnesota where I had gone to high school. We settled on Oberlin because it gave the opportunity to study lots of different things. At the time I was passionate about at least a dozen different things and had no idea what I was going to do for a career. Naturally I wanted to put off that decision for as long as possible, hoping I would figure it out during college.

I was always interested in technology, but before starting college (and also during a fair amount of college itself) my leanings were toward art and writing. That's not to say I didn't spend a ton of time in front of screens — my unofficial babysitters were my Gameboy, Nintendo, and PC running Windows 2000 —but as a kid my best friend was an extremely talented artist. Drawing together was one of our favorite past times. I loved to go to museums and could stare at my friend's art for hours. I also loved to read and wrote numerous short stories in middle school. I also wrote for my high school paper.

Basically, I was a creative generalist and loved all things that involved the imagination. However, my parents kept pushing me toward a practical path, because they were still struggling with their own careers and worried about employment options for creatives in the USA. Of course they were right to worry, since very few artists succeeded in getting their work into a gallery, let alone selling that work for enough money to make a living. However, I learned in my late teens that there was another option- which sounded much more practical than being a writer or an artist. It was an area of overlap between art and the internet, and it was called web design.

I dabbled in web design during middle school and high school, when I participated in roleplaying forums and later decided to create my own which had a very generic look that I wanted to modify. Essentially it was just a monochrome colored forum with no background images or icons, and I wanted the forum to look like it was part of the website where I described the world the roleplay took place in. I wanted the design to fit the mood of the world.

Essentially I was using CSS to make these changes. Unfortunately it was back when there was no such thing as developer tools (which would allow you to see the CSS alongside the site and actually make modifications to see the visual changes in real time) and no documentation. So the level of frustration accompanied with something as benign as altering the background color was shockingly time consuming. Despite all that, I enjoyed the challenge and it was fun and rewarding to see my websites come to life.

By the time I was starting college I was thinking web design was a pretty likely career option. Then I found out that Oberlin does not actually have a design degree. What it did have was a creative writing degree, one of the best undergraduate creative writing programs in the country. If I had known that my future would be pretty much solely focused on web development, I probably would not have given Oberlin another glance.

Though I knew art was probably not much of a viable career, I thought maybe if I got into the creative writing program I could become a successful writer. All thoughts of design and technology basically went out the window at this point. There was still a part of me that hoped to become a bestselling author, and that snowflake wasn't going to melt so easily. I suppose the snowflake never fully melted, since I am writing this book.

It took a number of events in college for me to revisit web design. The first was that I was never accepted into the creative writing program, the second was the economic recession which happened while I was at Oberlin, and the third was breaking up with my long distance boyfriend, who had a tendency to put down my technical skills because he was insecure about his own.

Even as I continued to take art and design classes, I began to wonder if it was the right path for me. I enjoyed aspects of it, such as the strategic thinking that was necessary to identify audience and tone. But the 2D limitations of the medium frustrated me, and my classmates and professors who were more interested in conceptual work didn't always mesh with my desire to master craft.

I wondered if I could do more with design if I learned how to code. I also wondered if a career in design was going to be sufficient to make a living wage. I was hearing from friends and acquaintances that they couldn't find a job. The future was starting to look a lot scarier than it had before. It seemed that technology was a major threat to many other fields. Though I had never doubted this before, when I looked at designer portfolios online I could hardly find any that were made by beginners. I was extremely intimidated by the senior design portfolios that I came across, and wasn't sure that I would have what it took to compete. I even considered transferring to another school.

It wasn't until I got a job working for the Oberlin Office of Communications that some of my fear about post college life was assuaged. If you are in college or soon to be starting college, I highly recommend that you also find some sort of part time employment. I did all sorts of things and learned a lot about myself in the process, possibly more than I learned from all the classes I took combined.

I did some freelance work as a graphic designer, and this taught me how to work with people in different age groups and what it was like being in a client-contractor relationship. It also showed me that freelance work involved being very good at navigating different personalities and clearing up any confusion, while also putting your foot down repeatedly. In addition there was the age old mantra: the customer (or client) is always right. That meant that even if I knew a design decision might turn out to look poorly, I often had to make compromises for the sake of pleasing the client. It also meant that sometimes

I might have to change something I was really proud of because the client didn't like it.

Here is a list of some of the other jobs I took while in college: obituary writer, photographer, interviewer, dance instructor, and archives assistant. I hope this helps to illustrate that people come into tech from all sorts of backgrounds, and there is not one clear cut path. I've met women who used to be social workers, physical therapists, filmmakers, and everything in between.

Takeaways

Not everyone who enters programming goes to college. I went to college, but much of what I learned there did not directly apply to my future career. Non traditional students come from all sorts of backgrounds, and by talking about my degree I am not trying to imply that it is necessary to get a job as a developer. In fact, it is not necessary at all.

What is necessary, however, is a passion for learning. That is the main thing I got out of college, and the main thing that I think is important to understand for those thinking about entering the field. In front end development especially, there is a new framework to learn every couple of years. So feeling comfortable with learning new things and not hesitating to ask questions when you have them are crucial skills.

There are many ways to practice learning how to learn. As a non traditional developer, you will probably end up teaching yourself a lot of the skills to get your first job. It's important to know what techniques help you learn best. I learned in college that it's easier for me to master new information when I can translate it visually. In the absence of that, I learn better if I am writing my own notes as the teacher is talking, especially if I translate it into my own words.

Another important thing I learned in college was time management. Especially during my programming classes, which I talk about in the next chapter, I had to get pretty good at estimating how long the homework would take me, and stay disciplined on the weekends to get it done.

I don't know if I would have had the discipline to get through my classes without the support of my professors. That is the nice thing about college: you get in-person mentorship and structure to get through your work. But there are plenty of students in college who spend their time at parties, neglecting their assignments, and simply failing to pass their classes. So obviously college is not the answer for everyone. It's also very expensive, especially in the case of liberal arts colleges like Oberlin.

What I'm trying to say is that it's important to get those basic skills and knowledge about yourself and how you learn before you sink in to any serious programming training—especially if you are considering something like a boot camp where you have to stay dedicated to your work for three months straight, with longer hours than your standard 9-5. Picking the right courses and learning approach is crucial, as my next story will hopefully illustrate.

My own husband experienced the problem of taking the wrong course for his learning style and sadly, never gave programming another chance since. He graduated with a degree in history and was feeling lost after college, not knowing what career to pursue. He took some classes in psychology in Cleveland and volunteered with Spanish-speaking immigrants at an organization downtown. I suggested that he try learning to code, because I knew he was determined and hard working enough (he now works as an attorney and graduated from Georgetown Law University).

I regret that I encouraged my husband to take the course without taking a more careful look at the content. The biggest problem was that the course switched gears dramatically halfway through, from teaching C to teaching Javascript, two completely different languages. For someone like my husband, who dislikes sudden shifts in general, this was devastating. I will get into more detail in the next chapter, where I'm going to talk specifically about my programming classes.

2

Programming Classes

Memories

After building my confidence in freshman year I decided to take advantage of my liberal arts school flexibility, and enroll in my first programming class. The thing I remember feeling most at the beginning was surprise. For some reason I expected programming would involve spending a lot more time with the hardware of the computer, and needing to understand how the most primitive parts of a computer worked. That is to say, I thought that I needed to know how to take a computer apart and how to put it back together, and be able to explain how each piece of the computer functioned in order to translate code.

Since nobody had ever given me any clue about what being a programmer was actually like, I really had no idea. I slowly learned that all my preconceptions were incorrect. Even math was not something that I needed to be super adept with. Programming simply adhered to rules which, once understood, were applied in a straightforward manner to pretty much all programming languages. At its core was something I felt like I could master: logical thinking.

It was honestly my first real exposure to seeing code on a screen. I had never been exposed to it in elementary, middle, or high school, nor was it ever mentioned by any teacher, coordinator, or camp counselor in my entire life. This fact, now that I look back on it, ought to have been the most shocking one of all. I had certainly been exposed to math and science, but to this day I cannot believe that nobody had so much as entertained the thought of showing me how to code when I was younger.

My first programming class was pretty much an introduction where we learned Python, a language which very much resembles English. In retrospect I probably could have skipped it and dove right into the larger and more intense Java programming class that funneled students into the Computer Science major. Instead, and because I had very little self esteem and had been told hundreds of time over my life that programming was "hard, challenging, and probably not for me", I took the less intimidating path. If you identify as a woman (or any marginalized group in tech), that will probably sound familiar.

In the Java class, I spent about a dozen hours each week on the take home projects. This paid off greatly and helped to balance out my grade when I didn't do so well on the exams. It also meant that the vast majority of my time during that semester was spent on programming assignments. This was the first time I realized just how extremely frustrating and challenging it can be to get something to work with your code, but also my first time experiencing the elation of having a functional program that I created with my own hands.

This elation was especially strong when I got to create the Go Fish game with Java. Since I loved to play games as a kid, making a game felt like going behind a magical curtain. I had never imagined that I would have the ability to actually create those experiences that brought me so much joy in my childhood that they felt truly special. It was such an empowering feeling to create something from scratch that people could interact and play with. Like one of my friends told me years later, programming has a certain element of magic. I loved the feeling of being the magician, and creating something that seems to have a life of its own.

Despite this elation, like the vast majority of my female peers at college, I decided not to pursue a Computer Science major. I heard lots of horror stories about how the next class I would have to take was extremely challenging. That it involved data structures far more complex than arrays or classes, and that I would be lucky if I passed. So even though I would have had a perfect A in my Java programming class were it not for a few pesky exams (I got an A on every take home assignment), I was scared that I would fail the data structures class.

Nobody attempted to dissuade me from that decision. Not even my parents, because they were worried it would be too stressful for me. It seemed perfectly natural that I chose to pursue design and the arts with a bit of programming sprinkled in, rather than the other way around. If I had decided to stay in the major, I would have been the only other woman graduating with a Computer Science degree in my year.

This "sprinkle" of Computer Science ended up being a 12 credit concentration as part of my Visual Arts degree, which was one of those strange creatures one can only find in a liberal arts college. Most of the credits toward my degree came from the Art Department, but I could choose 12 credits from any other department to supplement my degree and call it my concentration.

I was lucky that there were some Computer Science classes that I could take outside the track towards the major. Not all of the classes really added to my knowledge of programming. 3D Animation, for example, was a fun class but was more useful for learning 3D software and modeling skills than writing code. I basically skirted around the difficult classes and took the easier ones that I could find.

I should have realized back then after how much fun I had in my programming classes, despite their difficulty, that it was more useful and more practical for me to continue with the full Computer Science degree. On the other hand, taking those art classes helped me to explore my creative side. I still have mixed feelings about my decision, because I do miss expressing myself creatively sometimes. But back in college my decision was fueled more by fear. I chose what at the time felt like the safer, more comfortable path. I didn't necessarily regret this decision, but I sometimes wonder what would have happened if I hadn't been scared away from majoring in Computer Science.

In a perfect world I wanted to work on games, which was the perfect blend of art and programming. From that perspective my choice to major in Art with a concentration in Computer Science makes more sense. Maybe if I had moved to California I would have even gotten a job like that. I had no idea that in large swaths of the country jobs that merged creativity and technology were few and far between.

It was in my junior year I that I finally started revisiting the possibility that I could be a software engineer after college. I was tired of being at the whim of my clients and missed some of the problem solving that I got to do when I wrote code. I realized that I thought that I had been too weak to work in the field of software engineering, because of sexism and because I was non traditional and also because I was sensitive and creative and all of the things that a tech bro was not. I also realized that these were all stereotypes that provided no indication of my actual competence as a developer.

Ironically, the final straw was no big accomplishment in tech that made me realize how wrong I had been. It was actually because I had just done something I never thought I could do… break up with my boyfriend despite my issues with codependency and lifelong fear of rejection. If I could do that, then who knows what else I was capable of?

Even with that extra confidence, I was afraid of the future. With economic turmoil looming, my parents' anxiety about my career, and by extension my own, increased. I could see the anxiety among my classmates as well; the closer we got to graduation the more it could be seen. I also felt guilty that my parents were paying for this expensive college, and I still wasn't sure that I could pay it all back. Would it all have been worth it, in the end?

I applied for some developer jobs in my last year of college, but sadly none of them accepted me. Like many people graduating college after the recession, I had to settle for what I could get. If someone had told me in high school what my first job out of college would be I may not have believed them. It wasn't a design job, or a programming job, or a writing job. In addition, the "where" was equally surprising as the "what". I was going to be staying in the same tiny town where I had gone to college for another two years. I was going to be an "Art Technical Coordinator."

Takeaways

My programming classes in college were only the beginning. It was not enough to qualify me for any web development jobs, as I mentioned. However, it did lay the groundwork that made it easier for me to pick up new languages like Javascript. There is a big difference between the programming courses that offer you foundational knowledge about concepts like variables, for loops, if statements, and data structures and courses that cover the nuances of a specific language or framework.

Once you master the foundational concepts, it will be much easier to go on to some of those other more niche courses. The hard part is sorting through all of the existing courses and learning materials out there to find something that suits you.

Even though my programming classes were focused on building that foundation of knowledge, they were still not perfect for my learning style. A lot of material for my Java class was presented in a lecture format with long presentations in a large auditorium. It was early in the morning and I have never been a morning person, so I often missed the first few minutes of class.

Because of the large auditorium setting, I never felt comfortable raising my hand or asking questions in class. Even after class, I didn't want to wait in line to ask a question because there was usually several students waiting to talk to the professor after class.

In addition, the large class size coupled with the less than engaging lecture format made it tempting for me to goof off on my computer or my phone. I didn't do it often, but it was enough to miss some of the material which was probably part of the reason I ended up not doing well on my exams.

Speaking of exams, there is a lot of controversy around how well an exam can really gauge someone's understanding of programming. Kind of like the debate around white board interviews, where the programmer must write code on a white board, it is perceived by many to be outdated and ineffective. I am inclined to agree, because writing code on a piece of paper or a white board just throws you out of the mindset you are in when you are programming.

Even with all of these downsides, I still think I learned a lot in my programming classes in college. They were actually more challenging than the coursework I took later online, because Javascript is a more flexible language and doesn't force you explicitly declare things the same way that Java does.

3

The Ranks of the Employed

Memories

I first learned about the Art Technical Coordinator position a few months before I graduated, when I finished my Senior Studio art exhibit and was wrapping up loose ends before receiving my diploma. When I read the long list of requirements and duties for the job, combined with the rather low pay, I was ambivalent.

On the other hand, it was tempting to work somewhere that I felt comfortable, and the art department was almost like my home away from home. Things also had not gotten any easier with the economic depression and none of the developer or design jobs I applied to were giving me so much as a phone interview.

The art department was going to interview me in person right off the bat, and there were only 3 other candidates. I had worked with nearly all of the professors in some capacity and felt like I knew them. It didn't hurt my chances that I was a quiet, studious student. I had few friends in the art department with whom to be disruptive, and I had always been paranoid about my grades.

The position also required a lot of technical expertise, like knowing how to use the Adobe Creative Suite, being able to calibrate printers and maintain lab computers while providing general technical support to professors and students alike. As you can probably guess I had a lot of these credentials from my assortment of jobs.

All of the art department professors were present for the interview, which took me by surprise seeing that the position was low profile and mostly involved helping out just two of the professors (media arts and photography). Although I had prepared for some of their questions, the preparation didn't help very much.

I learned that sometimes the people interviewing you don't know how to phrase a question, and there is no shame in asking them to repeat themselves or rephrase what they are asking. There were some awkward moments, but I learned it is better to ask questions than try to answer something you don't understand.

When I got the job offer I felt some relief. Certainly, I was flattered that the art professors liked me so much, but I also felt some disappointment. As a kid I saw becoming an adult as being my path to freedom. It was a reality check to realize how much work needed to be done for me to be qualified for the types of jobs I really wanted. The whole "get a degree then get a job" thing wasn't really working out the way I was told it would from teachers and mentors growing up. *Follow your dreams! Don't give up! Reach for the stars!* What if this was all there was? Could I really achieve more?

This fear that web development jobs would be forever out of my reach grew deeper as I started my new job. Based on the many responsibilities listed in my job description, I thought that I would be extremely busy. It would be a lesson that I would have to learn again and again in future positions; job descriptions don't accurately reflect what you do on a day to day basis at work. In fact, there were jobs even in tech where I would find myself bored out of my mind. Luckily my position as Art Technical Coordinator was not that bad. In fact, though I hadn't realized it yet, the free time was actually a blessing in disguise.

Unfortunately, at first I was very frustrated. I was kept busy some days with a variety of tasks such as calibrating monitors and printing posters or fixing computers, but there was a far greater quantity of time where I had nothing to do at all. I was used to having some external motivator to get work done, usually in the form of grades. Now if I wanted to do anything extra, the only motivation had to be within me. And the only person that would know I accomplished anything would also be: just me. It was the first time that nobody else seemed invested in what I was doing. That made it extra hard to force myself to work on anything beyond what my job required.

I had expected my job to give me purpose, to make me feel like I was contributing in some important way. Something more than impressing my teachers and proving to my parents that I wasn't an idiot. It was extremely distressing to me when I came to the realization that the daily grind of school was being replaced with nothing better than the daily grind of work. In some ways the work grind was even worse. At least in school there had been a variety of tasks, teachers who cared about me, classmates that shared my workload, and a general sense of camaraderie.

It wasn't all bad though. My first job out of college did help me to build my confidence. For instance, I got to see what it was like to be a leader in the classroom. Although there had been plenty of times friends had asked me for help, I had never experienced being looked up to in a professional context. Students trusted me to help them with their technical problems. It was the first time I felt like my knowledge had value. I was shocked to see that some students actually looked up to me and were grateful for my help. This was mind boggling because just a year earlier I had been a student myself. The respect with which I was treated made it easier for me to assert myself later when I had my first developer job.

I had one student who would come in every week to work on her video art, and she often chatted with me for hours about her project. I would give her pointers on the best software to use to accomplish her artistic vision. Another student would come to me regularly for help with her animation project which she was doing for an independent study.

I also felt like I had done something to actually earn that respect. I had to prepare workshops and show students that I knew what I was talking about. Sometimes it was stressful because I never knew what a student might ask me. What if I didn't know the answer? I didn't cope very well with that stress, nor with the fluctuations in my schedule. I still remember some of my failures quite vividly.

There was a time a student came needing to print and bind an art book and I ended up wasting a bunch of paper and printing the colors in her images all wrong. I did not have that much experience with printing yet and she had showed up last minute not really understanding how complicated of a process printing could be. I felt frustrated that I couldn't help her but also annoyed that the student had ignored all my guidelines and instructions not to procrastinate on the printing process.

Another time I was tasked with creating a book of letters for a retiring art professor. The book needed to be interspersed with images from the professor's students, and designed to reflect the art professor's minimalist design aesthetic. I worked on the book for at least a month, and tried to make it as nice as I could. The problem was that everyone wanted to have a say about what went in the book, and many of the alumni didn't hand in their letters to the professor until past the deadline. In order to get the book printed in time, I could not possibly fit all of the contributions that were submitted after the deadline. At the end of it all, the retiring professor didn't seem very happy with what I created.

But worse than the failures were the times when I sat in my office not sure what to do with myself, feeling like this was going to be my whole future. When I helped a student with an important project or when a professor was frantically trying to fix their computer to meet a deadline and needed my help, I felt some kind of fulfillment. I knew I should follow this feeling. Still, for every hour of fulfillment there were times when I sat for hour upon hour alone. Those hours were painful, and I knew I needed something to fill that time-void. I needed to have a next step, a goal to strive towards.

Takeaways

There are probably thousands of people right now bored at work. Maybe they spend hours of their day browsing Reddit or Facebook or Instagram, not very happy with their job but also scared of quitting. Maybe one of those thousands of people is you. It sucks. In a weird way, all those hours doing nothing saps away your energy more than if you had real work.

Or you could be in a different boat. Maybe your job is boring, but you can't browse the internet during those hours. Maybe you are a food service worker or an Amazon warehouse employee. You work long, physically exhausting hours.

I was lucky that my job not only had hours of free time but also that I had my own office where nobody was breathing down my neck. Even if someone did catch me, I could justify the hours I spent learning Javascript by saying that it was for the purpose of becoming a better mentor to the students in the media lab. There weren't a lot of web related classes taught in the department, but enough that it was still relevant.

If you're in the first group of people I mentioned and spend time during your day browsing the internet, you are in the best position to utilize some of that time to begin your coding training. Let's be honest, if your boss doesn't care about you being on Facebook or Reddit, then your boss can hardly complain if you are reading coding tutorials instead.

Of course it's harder if you are in the second group and need to be on your feet all day. The last thing you will want to do after a long day of physical labor is more work. For those of you in this position, I suggest considering doing a bit of coding in the morning or on your way to work. Long commute? Listen to a coding podcast for beginners. Allowed to listen to music while you work? A podcast works in that scenario too.

The thing about physically difficult jobs is that coding doesn't involve any physical labor, so as long as your mind still feels fresh you can probably still knock out a small tutorial or training exercise every day. It's not as ideal as having free time where you can comfortably sit down for hours and work at something, but it's still not the worst case scenario.

The worst situation is when your job is both mentally draining and time consuming. You don't have a lot of extra time in your day, and even if you do your brain already feels fried and you have zero motivation to write code after all of that stress.

If you are in this category, I have a few suggestions. One option is getting a different job that is less challenging but still in the field you have already mastered. Maybe the pay is a little bit less, but the trade off in free time will be well worth it. Look for desk jobs, especially the boring sounding regular ones. Remember, if it doesn't work out you can always go back to that old job. Nobody can take your old credentials away from you.

Another option is switching to part time work, or leaning on a spouse/family member for a period of time. If you pick this option, make sure you give yourself a time limit. It's easy to just fall into complacency if you don't have a bit of structure or a goal you're trying to reach. Trying to convince a family member to let you live with them without paying your fair share may be a hard bargain unless you give them some reassurances that it won't end up a permanent arrangement.

Of course my earlier advice about listening to a podcast during your commute or while you are working on a more tedious task still applies. You can do this even if you have a more mentally draining job without a lot of free time. There are probably still slower periods even if you work in one of those demanding types of fields.

4

Early Mentors

Memories

One of the people who helped me get through those two years the most was Jim. Jim wasn't actually his real name, but he was a private kind of guy so I am not using his real name here. He was hired to manage the technical resources of the Cinema Studies department, which had just finished building a top notch recording and filming studio above the old movie theater in town. Jim was a big asset to the department because he had a sound design degree, and was probably the only person in the entire college that knew how to use all the tools inside the recording studio.

Though his primary responsibilities were within Cinema Studies, Jim also oversaw the equipment in the Art Department. This proved to be quite difficult because the departments didn't really want to share their resources, and were mostly being forced to by the college. It was lucky that Jim was a very likable and diplomatic guy, but even so it made his job less than easy.

Jim also assisted me with getting through some of the most confounding projects the professors threw at us, and was very pragmatic when it came to discussions around finding my purpose and accomplishing my professional goals. Over the course of many coffees at the local Slow Train café, Jim told me about the array of jobs he'd had since his graduation with a degree that (somewhat like mine) had not opened up many doors. He had worked in a pizza shop with his parents, as part of the crew on a yacht, and even worked a graveyard shift converting film audio for airplane listening.

Jim had the unfortunate timing of graduating just a few years before the economic crash, so he saw firsthand how the system caved in on itself. He told me how before the depression he was getting interviews without a whole lot of effort, but after it was like pulling teeth and the number of interviews he would get got cut by more than half.

Jim's experience taught me that there was really no direct path to career success, or figuring out where I belonged. What I would inevitably need was lots of different experiences, and the patience to keep tallying up the results until something clear came into view. He revealed to me just how many of my assumptions about life after college were wrong.

One of the biggest assumptions I had was that jobs are created only when there is a real and serious need. Growing up I never heard my parents complain about being bored at work, so I had always assumed that work involved long hours and painstaking effort. I didn't stop to think about how need in any organization is based on perception rather than reality. Or how people might inflate responsibilities for a position to get a little extra help, among other motivations.

For Jim, the gaps in our schedule were a blessing rather than a curse. He would find things to do with his free time, working on his experimental instruments (he was quite talented with woodworking) and learning new skills that he thought might make him more useful to the professors. Although I could not quite adopt his laissez faire approach, and sometimes we would have the conversation again and again without getting closer to a resolution, he was part of the reason I decided to teach myself Javascript despite the lack of any obvious opportunities in sight.

Even though my job as an Art Technical Coordinator was pretty lax, I was pretty sure the tech industry would be different. It would take hard work to get myself there. Maybe in the past college would have prepared me with the skills I needed to succeed, but that was not true anymore. I needed to be like Jim and take advantage of my free time to learn the skills I needed to put me in the career I wanted.

Takeaways

You might be wondering why I dedicated a chapter to discussing a mentor who is working as an engineer or CTO or even UX designer. The thing is, even though I did have a few meetings with developers in my two years working for my alma mater, those people didn't work with me on a regular basis or have the time to share the progression of their career with me in detail.

Jim's enthusiasm and willingness to tackle any problem was inspirational, especially when we were dealing with old stubborn computers or blue screens of death. It wasn't uncommon to spend hours trying to fix one machine. Sometimes writing code really isn't that different from working in IT. You can't memorize all of the answers, and google is always your friend. If you're easily frustrated you might find that coding is not for you.

So even though Jim couldn't offer me any insider knowledge on coding best practices or how to get my foot in the door, he was the perfect role model for what kind of attitude I should have as I approach a career as a developer. No matter what new project was thrown our way he was quick to dive in and get his hands dirty.

One really good example of this was when Jim ordered a printer for the new screen-printing professor. Because Jim was working with a strict budget, he ended up buying an older model that was on sale. When it arrived I was tasked with connecting it to the network so students could print from their own laptops. I knew virtually nothing about the topic and grew frustrated pretty quickly as I tried to setup the printer.

When Jim arrived a few hours later the energy changed in the room. I briefed him about what I had attempted so far. He sat down and calmly took in my rambling explanation. Even though I was already on the verge of giving up, Jim didn't allow my frustration to phase him. The thing is, Jim didn't have any experience working with networks or setting up old printers either. He just approached new problems with curiosity instead of fear or doubt.

Not only was Jim patient with old hardware and IT problems, he also tackled new projects of his own volition to assist students. One good example of this was when one of the seniors wanted to have an interactive artwork that played audio when someone walked in front of it. Jim had heard of something called an Arduino that was essentially a very small computer that you could plug sensors into and program to trigger a response.

Essentially Jim had just dove headfirst into a coding project, because once we plugged in the sensors it was necessary to actually write some code to tell the Arduino device what to do when it detected interaction. He looked at documentation and stack overflow as well as GitHub to gather together tidbits of code until he was able to figure out how to get the program working.

I didn't know it at the time, but this was the most inspirational quality about Jim, and what gave him the mentality of a programmer. They never have all of the answers, and they often have to research and piece things together to get a program working. I can't tell you how many times in my programming career I ended up stuck on a problem for hours or even days and just had to maintain a positive attitude, breaking down issues into smaller components until I figured it out.

I guess what I'm ultimately trying to say is that mentors come in all shapes and sizes, and sometimes the people you remember helping you the most are not the experts or the friends with the connections. Sometimes mentors can be more like comrades in arms, who inspire you to keep going with your projects and not give up even in the face of adversity. Sometimes they show you the difference between a productive approach and a destructive one.

Either way, I encourage you to look for mentors with this advice in mind, and remember that your mentors may be staring you in the face. Don't be afraid to ask them for help and advice. A good mentor should be open and willing to assist you. Sometimes you might be scared to talk to them, but if they disparage you they are not the right person. Everyone was a beginner at some point, and sometimes successful developers let their success get to their heads. So don't be discouraged if those types of developers aren't helpful, it simply means they lack the skills for mentorship.

5

Teaching Myself

Memories

I wish I could say that my path to learning Javascript and creating a programming portfolio was an organized one. As someone who always had a messy desk and too many thoughts in her brain, I was envious of some of my friends and peers with their mood boards and their planners all perfectly laid out.

My messy desk very much reflected the chaos in my brain as I approached the task of transforming myself into "someone who had taken a couple coding classes" into "someone who looked like a qualified developer." At the time it felt like an impossible feat, because I had very little information on what a qualified developer looked like.

As I'm sure any woman reading this book can relate, there are not a lot of role models in this field for us to look up to or give us guidance on how you become a developer, or what sort of trials you might face. It is no small part of the reason why I decided to write this book, though I am glad to say the situation has improved significantly even in just the last five years.

It would be impossible for me to tell you exactly what order I ended up tackling my projects, but I do have a general memory of the resources I used and what I was measuring myself against. Honestly my biggest obstacle was always my own self doubt, and the fact that the more I learned, the more I discovered how many frameworks and languages and tools there were, and the more insecure I became.

In order to avoid being swallowed up by the weight of it all, I decided I would focus on a very specific niche of programming: games. It made sense on multiple levels: I was very familiar with games, they were fun, allowed me to be creative, and I would have a project at the end of it to put in my portfolio that I would feel proud to show off.

At this point I hadn't explored Javascript too much, but I had an inkling that I wanted to work primarily on the web, so learning Javascript would be a prerequisite. I was very lucky that I still had full access to the myriad of resources that my alma mater provided by being an employee of the college.

These resources included a free subscription to Lynda, access to the massive library of tech publications on Safari Books, and multiple physical libraries on campus. Of those three resources, I would say the most helpful was probably Safari Books. While Lynda had a tremendous choice of different classes, the fact that I had to constantly pause the video, switch screens, write some code, and then switch back again.

That back and forth routine became very tedious very quickly. It might not have been a problem if I had a second monitor at my disposal, but with one small laptop screen I needed most of that real estate to see my code. Shrinking the video to only take up half the screen made everything too small so I had no choice but to keep pausing and toggling.

The Lynda courses I remember most was one that covered MYSQL and PHP and another one that covered mobile game development with Javascript and HTML5 (relatively new at the time). The former course was honestly quite boring, because it involved making a simple web application for managing your own website. Like Wordpress but without all the bells and whistles. I had to build an admin page, a login page, a database for handling the user information, and of course actual pages for users to create, display, update, and delete.

Even though that class didn't involve much Javascript, I didn't know exactly what I needed to learn at the time to get a job as a developer. So, I thought it would be useful to know at least some back end functionality. I turned out to be wrong because almost all of my roles ended up being front end focused and hardly ever using PHP. On the other hand, the project still involved writing code and still made it easier to do my future projects.

The mobile game development project was more useful in terms of actually involving writing Javascript. Calling it mobile game development is a bit of a stretch. I was not writing code native to a mobile phone, but rather designing the game so that it would fit the size of the small screen and be easy to play on a phone. It would be more accurate to call it a web game, because you had to open a web browser to play it properly.

That being said, the game was a lot more fun to make and felt more rewarding than when I completed the Wordpress imitation. It was called Bunny Defender and basically involved frantically tapping around the screen to destroy asteroids before they hit the bunnies that populated your planet.

Building those first few projects was empowering, but I knew

I had to do more before I felt like I could tackle my own project. I was beginning to get frustrated with the back and forth toggling on Lynda between video and code, so I decided to look into another platform for tech training: Safari Books.

Running a search for web games on the ebook library was exciting and overwhelming. I immediately got hundreds of results, much more than what was available on Lynda. The only problem was that you still had view the book in your browser. If I had a physical copy, I could just have that book open next to my laptop. So I still had the problem of needing to have multiple windows open in the limited real estate of my laptop screen.

At the end of the day, it was still better than Lynda videos. I was able to keep the last page of the text open next to my code rather than needing to rewind a video if I forgot some portion of what I needed to do. I also found a book that was perfect for me: a step by step manual to build a number of different web games with Javascript.

These days its pretty uncommon to teach beginner coders much about plain Javascript. Students jump pretty quickly into frameworks like React or Angular. This was also before ES6, so plain Javascript was a lot funkier and had much fewer shortcuts than it does today. The first game I made is actually still on my Github page.

This game was called alien attack and it involved guessing the coordinates of a little alien in a grid. Every time you typed in your guess, a little rocket launcher would move to those coordinates and try to shoot the alien. This was my first time using CSS to create simple animations.

Even though the instructions were handed to me much the same way they were in a Lynda tutorial, I felt much more accomplished when I completed the alien attack game than when I completed the bunny defender game. Perhaps because it was easier for me to attempt to figure things out on my own. I would stop reading and think about the solution, but a video would just keep playing and give me the answer before I had a chance to think about it. That way I felt like I learned more, and like I was starting to retain knowledge.

Finally I decided it was time to tackle my own project. I should emphasize I still had so little confidence in myself at this point, despite all those tutorials I completed. Part of me resisted actually making my own game, and it wasn't easy to push that resistance down. I managed it by taking baby steps. There was a 15 puzzle game I made in the same book I mentioned earlier, but it was just with simple number blocks. It occurred to me I could make the game more interesting by scrambling an image instead of numbers.

This would involve getting the right size image, dividing it into equal size squares, and then scrambling it so that the player would have to solve the resulting puzzle. It was the perfect challenge that wasn't as intimidating as building something from scratch but still required me to do some problem solving of my own. Coincidentally, it's also still on my GitHub account.

For a while after completing the 15 scramble puzzle I was stuck. I knew I wanted to make another game, but I didn't want to make something that already had hundreds of existing copies. Putting a new face on a game like Candy Crush or Tetris or any number of popular arcade games just didn't seem like it would be that rewarding. I was also never a big fan of mobile games so I felt like maybe that wasn't the best option.

It was actually my husband who gave me the idea for the game I would finally make. He was writing a trilogy at the time, based on a medieval but fantastical type of world. His main character was a woman who wanted to become a warrior, and my husband wanted her to become fascinated with a game that imitated military strategy. During his google searches he came across a game called Hnefatafl.

Hnefatafl is an ancient viking board game that predates chess and is meant to mirror the positioning of two armies facing off. The white pieces represent an army surrounded on all sides by a larger army of black pieces. For white, the goal is to get their king (in the center of the board) to one of the four corners representing a safe escape. For black, the goal was to corner the king on all four sides, thereby defeating the white army.

I won't get into all of the details of the game, but suffice it to say that the mechanics were somewhat similar in terms of complexity to checkers. When I went online to see if anybody else had made a web version of the game, I was pleased to find that very few existed. The ones that did either failed to show where the pieces could move, or had a pretty poor user interface. I knew that because of my design background I could make a version of the game that stood out from the others and would be easy for beginners to play.

It was by far the most challenging thing I decided to build thus far. What kept me going was this sense of excitement which grew and grew the further along I got. Unlike the other assignments I really felt a sense of ownership over what I was making. It was 100% mine and nobody could take that away from me. I felt so much pride when I completed that game, it is hard to put into words. But honestly, it was tackled in much the same way as my previous project. Breaking down the project into small pieces, having patience with myself, and taking a break whenever I felt stuck or frustrated.

Takeaways

Looking back on all of those classes I took, I think I could have benefitted from a more organized approach. I remember taking a class on another website called Treehouse using Ruby on Rails which not only did I never use again but the class itself was so outdated that I wasn't even able to complete the project.

These kinds of issues can also happen when you try to follow a tutorial on someone's blog. Make sure that any lessons you find aren't more than a few years old. Honestly, with the pace of web development I personally think even two years old is pushing it. A single missing or outdated dependency can make it impossible to run your app, and if you don't know what is missing you won't be able to fix it.

I say this from experience, because I also made this mistake. It was later in my career, when I already had a grasp of Angular and wanted to build a game with the framework. It's not really the kind of framework that lends itself well to making games so the only good example I could find was on someones blog. It was for making the popular game 2048 where you move numbers around a square board in one of four cardinal directions.

Every time you match the numbers, they go up by the power of the number you are matching. Eventually, if you match them enough times, you will reach the winning number: 2048. I was able to complete the main mechanics of the game following along with the blog instructions, though there were times when I had to go to stack overflow to fix outdated parts of the code.

The real problems started when I had to implement SASS mix-ins in order to create the animations for the squares. At this point they would simply teleport from left to right if the user clicked on the right arrow. SASS is a preprocessor to CSS (Cascading Style Sheets) which is used to set properties that define the look and feel of your web app.

No matter how hard I tried I couldn't get the SASS to work. I triple checked my code against the code written in the blog but it simply was not correct. After banging my head against the wall for a while longer, I eventually gave up and moved on to a different project.

Now there are a lot more ways to learn to code than there were when I was learning in 2014. There are free websites like Codecademy that let you read the instructions in a left hand panel, write the code in a center panel, and see the output of your code in a final panel on the right. Instructional websites like Codecademy eliminate the need to toggle between multiple windows completely. It's especially good for beginners.

Podcasts about coding (and just in general) have also become significantly more popular. I don't listen to a lot of podcasts myself but I know there are good ones out there, such as the Ladybug podcast where women in tech talk about how they got their start and offer advice to beginners. It's always inspirational and encouraging to listen to other peoples' stories, especially people you can relate to.

Another option that I wasn't aware of for learning to code when I was starting out is mobile apps. SoloLearn is one example. There are dozens of others, but SoloLearn is really good at breaking down coding concepts and practice challenges into small pieces that can fit on your phone's screen. Although you can't use SoloLearn while you are driving, you can complete an exercise during short waiting periods like while your morning coffee is brewing, or while you're waiting in line at the grocery store.

Yet another option is registering for a MOOC (Massive Open Online Courses). Basically traditional colleges and universities saw that online learning was becoming a popular alternative and started offering some of their courses to the public. Even very prestigious institutions such as Harvard offer some courses on MOOC platforms.

My personal favorite platform is Coursera. I enrolled in two specializations there, one about game development and another about interaction design. The former was four courses, while the latter was six. Both culminated in a capstone project where you actually had to create something for your portfolio that required applying all the knowledge you obtained in the previous courses.

The biggest difference between MOOCs and the other learning options is that at the end of each week you usually get an actual assignment from the professor of the class that you must complete. Much like a traditional class, that assignment will actually be graded (usually through ratings from your peers in the class). If that's not enough accountability, you can also pay to receive a certificate of proof that you completed the courses.

The only thing I would caution you about MOOCs is jumping into a course simply because of the prestigious institution that might have created it. Just because Harvard or MIT came out with a course about programming doesn't mean that it is automatically the best class for you to learn how to code. Remember that pacing yourself is important, and there is no shame in a slower pace if that means you will stick with it rather than giving up.

No matter how glitzy or impressive the course looks on the outside, make sure to do your research and read reviews before diving in. If there is a trailer or introduction that you can watch,

watch it. Does the instructor engage you? Does he speak too fast or too slow? Are there examples of assignments you can look at?

Also remember that different courses are geared toward different levels of experience. Don't enroll in an Angular or React course if you don't have any experience with Javascript. Likewise, if you've already taken a few Javascript courses don't be afraid of taking the plunge and trying out an Angular or React course.

Another thing I recommend is setting some learning goals and figuring out what areas you're most interested in. Don't try to learn back end and front end all at once. Don't jump from mobile development to web development either. It's easy to get overwhelmed in the world of programming so having an area of focus early on is key. Just because you find a course out there that looks cool doesn't mean you should enroll, unless it fits with your learning goals.

In many ways this is the hardest stage because you only have yourself and maybe a few friends or peers to hold you accountable as a self taught developer. It's unlikely you'll find much of support network in these online classes, so seek out real people to work on assignments with whenever possible. I say that because it will help keep you motivated, but also because you can teach each other things, which I believe is a great way to solidify your own knowledge. I will be talking about that and my own experience teaching in the next chapter.

6

Teaching Others

Memories

In the second year of my time working as an Art Technical Coordinator, my boss suggested that I consider teaching a Winter Term class. Winter Term was a concept that was somewhat unique to Oberlin, but also occurred on other liberal arts campuses. Each one had a different name but it was in essence the same. During the month of January, students didn't have any regular classes. Instead, they could enroll in special month long classes that were taught by other students, employees of the college, or even residents from town.

After getting some experience teaching workshops about Photoshop and Final Cut Pro and mentoring students the logical next step did seem to be offering a Winter Term class. The thing was, I had always been an anxious person. I was diagnosed with generalized anxiety disorder in college and sometimes the herbal remedies and breathing exercises were just barely enough to get me through the day.

Teaching a class was very much outside my comfort zone, but I was also bored with the daily routine and knew that if I didn't teach a class, I would have virtually nothing to do the entire month of January. Also I was less intimidated in front of a classroom than I used to be. My success with the Photoshop and Final Cut Pro workshops I taught convinced me that I could pull off teaching a Winter Term.

I didn't want to teach another class about Adobe products or other creative software. After all, I had been studying web development for nearly two years now. There were no classes taught on campus about web development, so it seemed like a natural choice to teach that in my Winter Term. The more difficult part was deciding what exactly within web development I should teach.

Javascript might be too difficult, especially because I would have students without any programming background whatsoever. HTML and CSS were the more obvious choices, but they were also hard to teach because they didn't follow any rules and require a lot of memorization.

I ended up settling on teaching HTML and CSS for the first two weeks of the Winter Term, and then pivoting to Wordpress and teaching students how they could customize their own Wordpress pages. In retrospect, I wasn't nearly as prepared as I thought I was. Teaching that class was the most intimidating thing I did as an Art Technical Coordinator, and I still feel a bit ashamed of some of what transpired during that month.

The first day of the class I was expecting students to ask me questions about the syllabus, and thought I would spend at least 15 to 30 minutes discussing the topics in the class. I completely underestimated how timid my students would be. They didn't have any questions so I ended up with over an hour to kill after reviewing the syllabus. I still remember that moment of terror when I had all those students staring at me waiting for me to say something and I had no idea what to do. Improvising was never my strong suit and I thought I had been prepared so it really caught me off guard.

When I decided the class should be two hours twice per week I assumed that students would need that time to work on their websites and would appreciate having me available for asking questions. I overestimated how much interest the students would have in web development. There were a few students who were really interested in the material but a lot of them showed up and did the bare minimum of work so they could pass.

Because the students didn't ask many questions and it was difficult for me to tell if they were really learning anything, I started giving them more activities like pairing with a partner to work on code together or completing tasks online. This worked better than what I was doing at the beginning. Sometimes I would have to explain things many times before they understood. It was frustrating for me because I had been expecting the students to be a little bit more engaged.

At the same time, I also had some really rewarding moments while teaching. One student completed an impressive and unique portfolio website that did a great job of showcasing her art. There was another student who would make inappropriate outbursts during class and she would let me know afterward how I shouldn't be afraid to silence him. This student would also often stay after class to talk to me about what she was working on. Watching her present her website made me proud to have taught that class and give her skills she could use in the future.

At the end of the day, I don't regret that I signed up to teach the class. Teaching gave me a new perspective on what its like on the other side of the classroom and how to be a better student. Even though I was done with college, being a better student also meant being a better mentee, and there were many companies still in my future where I would be mentored by more experienced developers and needed to be able to communicate effectively with them. I will talk about this and more reasons to practice being a teacher or mentor in the next section.

Takeaways

It might seem counterintuitive for me to talk about teaching when I haven't even gotten my first web development job yet. Sure, like me, you might have some basic knowledge about HTML and CSS and maybe you built a simple website or two, but you can't possibly be qualified to teach, right? That may seem like a logical conclusion, but it is in fact patently false.

Some of the best blogs and instructional materials out there on the internet right now were written by people who just learned the thing that they are teaching. Whatever the subject matter might be, you're usually best at teaching it when it's fresh in your mind. It astounded me when just six months ago, I volunteered to be a mentor at an introductory Javascript class and couldn't explain to a student why her code wasn't working.

It should have been easy; after all, the code was just a few dozen lines. The thing is, I had forgotten some of the basic concepts the students were working with because I hadn't touched them in years. That is because when you are programming at a company with enterprise applications your code is often working in multiple layers of abstraction that require understanding different concepts from the ones you learn when you are starting out.

I've worked with many developers who struggle to use plain language when explaining programming concepts, and get used to using terminology that makes it difficult or even impossible for a lay person to understand. It's not an easy skill, and developers can often feel discouraged from learning how to do it. This is because programmer fear making programming too accessible. After all, if it becomes a common skill the pay for programmers will go down and it might not be such a lucrative career anymore.

It's sad that so many programmers think this way but I have seen it time and time again in the industry. Some developers make their code convoluted on purpose because they believe it gives them job security. Others practice various forms of gatekeeping like white board interviews and degree requirements to intimidate prospective employees and make the job seem more challenging.

Being a good programming instructor requires being aware of all of these barriers to entry and explaining them to your students. It also requires avoiding the opposite extreme of telling students that programming is easy and everyone should do it. Like anything worth having, it takes hard work and dedication. It's a tough balancing act but without it, students won't have a realistic perspective of the industry.

Back to my actual point: teaching someone about programming will help you to understand the concepts better. The more you can communicate with plain language, the better you probably understand the concepts. Not to mention the more you practice explaining these concepts to a student or peer, the better you will be able to explain them in interviews. It's not uncommon for a prospective employer to ask an interviewee to explain programming concepts that are expected to be understood for the job.

One particularly popular teaching technique in the world of software development is known as peer programming. Basically, the student controls the computer while the mentor dictates what should be done. Whether it's adding a feature or fixing a bug, peer programming works because the student is typing the code and making the corrections themselves. A lot of companies advertise that they utilize peer programming but very few actually do it on a regular basis.

If you are good at peer programming you might actually find yourself mentoring programming students as a part time or even full time job. Between students enrolled in bootcamps and MOOCs and actual brick and mortar institutions there are thousands upon thousands of people who need help with their assignments every single day. Even with all of those existing options, the tech industry continues to complain about a shortage of talent so there is likely room for even more teachers still.

I hope I made it clear why practicing teaching early and often, even when you are just starting out learning about programming can be extremely beneficial. You don't have to immediately start teaching any classes or applying to be a mentor online but you can definitely practice explaining concepts to your friends or your family or even your dog. Just repeating things out loud can help to solidify your understanding. It's a great skill and you won't regret developing it.

7

Transition Anxiety

Memories

By the time I was wrapping up my second year of employment as an Art Technical Coordinator I had a pretty decent portfolio under my belt. I had built a robust game on my own, and had a bunch of games I built with the help of tutorials. I knew how to code static websites with HTML and CSS and even how to create mockups and UI elements in Photoshop. On top of that, I could put teaching a web development class on my resume.

A few months prior my husband had told me about a non-profit in his home city of Saint Louis called LaunchCode. It existed to help students enter the tech industry from non traditional backgrounds, offering mentoring and practice interviews and even recruiters who helped place students into local startups once they were proficient enough.

My husband and I had decided that six years was a long enough time to spend in a college town and we needed to move on. Neither of our positions had much room for upward mobility and Cleveland, the nearest major city, also lacked opportunities in the industries we were interested in. If we moved to Saint Louis we could live with my husband's family until we got our footing and save money. That was the plan, anyway.

Before we actually moved to Saint Louis I got in touch with a representative named Kelly from LaunchCode over email. We talked about my experience and Kelly thought that she could probably place me in a startup straight away. She even said that I could work remotely for them until I actually made the move to Saint Louis.

This seemed like a great idea because I could get to know my new coworkers a few months earlier and make some extra money while I was at it. The startup was very small, with only 3 full time employees and a handful of contractors. The majority of their work was with clients in the Saint Louis area building robust custom Wordpress sites.

Of course it wasn't as simple as just getting a recommendation from the recruiter. Like any job I still had to do an interview. I remember I was so anxious beforehand that I had to drink several cups of calming tea before my hands stopped shaking. It was the first sign that I had underestimated how much fear I had of switching industries and how much pressure I was putting on myself.

I don't recall many details from the actual interview, except that the interviewers clearly were not much more comfortable than me and didn't seem to really have a plan of what sort of questions to ask. In retrospect that should have been reassuring but it just made me more convinced that I was unqualified.

As a result I was quite surprised when I get a call a few days later from Kelly that I got the job. Although Wordpress was not my favorite platform to work with, I thought that since I had some Wordpress experience in the past it shouldn't be too difficult. What I underestimated was just how complex a Wordpress website could be and how many enterprise tools existed for managing multiple sites that I had never even heard of.

I still vividly remember my first on-boarding with the team. I needed to get set up with Github so I could see the code for the websites they were working with. Part of the process involves generating an SSH key on your machine with the terminal. I had never really done anything in the terminal before so I started getting anxious as soon as I had to open it up. It was also difficult to follow their instructions over video chat. The more times I had to ask for help and clarification, the more the panic began to build up. I remember apologizing profusely and feeling terrified and embarrassed, convinced that everyone on the call was judging me.

It didn't get any better after that either. I had told my boss that I was available for up to 10 hours a week but for several weeks they didn't have any work for me at all. Then without warning one day they asked me if I could help with some user interface elements. Of course it was terrible timing, the one day at work that week that I was busy. Sadly, I was too afraid to say no and jeopardize my position, so I said yes to the work even when I was not feeling comfortable.

Over the next few months I lived in fear of getting work assigned to me when I was busy. I hated that I never knew when the next project would pop up in my email. One day I had a video call with one of my supervisors. He told me that I should expect to receive an assignment in the next couple of hours. Instead of just going about my business for the day, I was so apprehensive that I sat in front of my computer obsessively refreshing my email.

I did that for at least three hours. I had a trip that evening and I was afraid my boss wouldn't reach out to me with the assignment until I was leaving and I would be forced to do it late at night. This fear was both irrational and overblown. First of all, if they did email me I could just say that I was busy on the weekend and would get to it on Monday. There was no reason for me to feel like I had to always say yes, because it was normal for contractors to have their own schedule and not have 24/7 availability.

Unfortunately I was too anxious at the time to see that. I began to believe that part time remote work was simply too stressful for me because I needed a set schedule and routine to feel comfortable. While that isn't entirely false, a big part of why it didn't work out was because of my own anxiety. I felt like I had to say yes to everything and never make a mistake or I would get fired. This led to a sense of crippling fear that ended with me deciding to quit the job.

After I quit, I decided I would see a psychiatrist and talk about my options. I realized I needed to spend some time focusing on my mental health rather than pushing myself harder. Anxiety was something I suffered from for a long time, but the career transition made it a lot worse. Thankfully after seeking treatment I began to feel a lot better. Much better than I had in many years, and much more mentally prepared for working at a startup.

Takeaways

I renamed this chapter several times and am still not sure I settled on the right title. Calling what I experienced while working part time for this web development company imposter syndrome would be a bit misleading, because imposter syndrome is often felt most deeply when you are working in person with people who are (usually) cis gender, mostly white, men. Being one of the only women or minority on the team often increases that sense of imposter syndrome a great deal.

The other reason I felt like imposter syndrome was the wrong word to describe how I was feeling is because one usually feels imposter syndrome after experiencing some significant success. If you've been hired as a software engineer or have been in the industry for several years and you still feel inadequate, you are certainly experiencing imposter syndrome. However if you are just starting out its trickier because you might believe that some of your inadequacy is real.

For what it's worth, I believe I was experiencing a mixture of imposter syndrome and anxiety symptoms. I had experienced some success by building a complex game on my own, and had the validation of receiving the job offer. So there were some signs of success, and yet I felt inadequate anyway. But beyond the inadequacy I also felt a tremendous amount of fear and dread.

It's entirely possible that you will also experience a spike in anxiety when you begin your career transition. All I can say is that you should try to stay aware of your mental health. It's easy to get so fixated on your performance at a new job that you sacrifice your well being. I suggest spending a little bit of time every day doing something that relaxes you. Not just a tv show or a video game, but something that releases all of the tension. It might be a massage, or meditation, or a hot bath. Take care of yourself.

Practicing self compassion is so important when you are beginning a career in tech. It's also a great way to combat imposter syndrome, because it requires acknowledging you are suffering and having compassion for yourself like you would if a cherished friend came to you with the same problems. You wouldn't tell a friend that they should just get over it or stop whining, so why tell things like that to yourself? Those negative thoughts can be a lot more harmful than we give them credit for.

Once you have a year or two of experience under your belt the anxiety about working with code will start to lessen. When you are struggling at the beginning and needing lots of guidance from your peers, remember that the situation is only temporary and you will learn and grow from all of your experiences. Every developer had to start somewhere, and there is no shame in being entry level.

To offer a real example, I've been working as a developer for four years now and I recently switched from working in Angular to React and Node. It's a huge transition and in many ways I feel like I'm starting all over again. Insecure and worried that I will frustrate my coworkers by asking too many questions. Even though I've been told again and again that I am competent and doing well at my job, those negative thoughts can still sneak up on me.

In some industries employees just learn a set of tools and solve the same kind of problems every day. As a developer, you are always tackling new problems and therefore there will always be more questions to ask. So embrace your own curiosity and push yourself to ask questions even when it feels uncomfortable. You will thank yourself later, I promise. I've been doing that in my current role and I am already feeling a lot better.

8

LaunchCode

Memories

After quitting my job with the tiny Wordpress startup I decided I wasn't going to worry about my career anymore until we were settled down in Saint Louis. I experienced a huge amount of relief after working with my psychiatrist on a treatment plan. Although I had resisted drugs for a long time I found that I had actually just been perpetuating my suffering and making myself miserable needlessly. All those years I spent being stubborn and fearing drugs was not worth it.

Moving to Saint Louis went pretty smoothly. In fact, it might have been the least stressful move in my entire life. Growing up I moved around a lot because my parents were reliant upon grant money for their research positions and if the grant money dried out, they were usually laid off. It felt horrible to be torn away from my friends and all the places I felt comfortable. Many times I would find myself feeling like a hollow shell, giving up the hope and sometimes even the desire to make new friends.

This time was completely different. I felt like there was nothing left for me in Oberlin. It was hard for me to relate to the college students or the professors, because neither were in my generation and both were in very different stages of their lives. The few young graduates who still lived there had their own social groups that I was not a part of. It felt like whatever resources or life lessons I had to learn from that place were all dried up, and it was time to move on to greener pastures.

It was the summer, so Saint Louis was in its prime with green grass and blossoming trees. My in-laws lived in a lovely historical home in a neighborhood where you could walk to shops, restaurants, and even the metro that could take you downtown. Though it was much smaller than DC where I would move to in a year's time, it had been the largest and nicest city I had ever lived in at that point.

Compared to Oberlin, where many of the students came from New York and weren't particularly welcoming, Saint Louis also felt full of friendly people. I still remember when I had started school in Oberlin and opened the door for a couple of other students as they were leaving a cafe. Not only did they not thank me for opening the door, they gave me sidelong glances of resentment. As someone who lived in the Midwest for most of her life, this really had not sat well with me.

The people that worked at LaunchCode mirrored the same type of Midwestern friendliness that put me at ease. Shortly after we moved, I made an appointment with them to assess my skillset and decide if I was good enough to place right away or if I could benefit from some more training. Normally I would have gone through that stage earlier, but because I had been remote they decided to wait until I moved to the area.

I remember being extremely nervous before meeting with

the LaunchCode staff. Even though I was told repeatedly that it was akin to a practice interview and actually there was only one person who would be assessing me, I felt like it was the first real technical interview I ever had. It was the first time I ever had to do a white board test. It was also the first time I actually had to explain how I completed one of my portfolio projects in detail.

The white board part of the test was definitely the most flabbergasting. I was surprised that this was actually a way many companies thought was appropriate to measure a programmers skill level. From the beginning it was like I had to channel a different part of my brain than what I actually use when I'm writing code on a computer. Maybe it's just me, but I maintain that there is something about the muscle memory of typing that makes writing code on a white board significantly more difficult.

Despite the stress of the practice interview, I performed well. Kelly contacted me later that week to let me know they felt that not only was I prepared to be placed with a local startup, but that they actually believed I was one of the top performers that they currently had looking for a job. This was probably the most validating thing I had heard, yet at the time I don't think the compliment really sunk in. I think that is because at the time I still had pretty low self esteem, and struggled with believing in myself and my abilities.

The fact that I was one of LaunchCode's top performers at that time put me in a unique position to be nominated for a hackathon sponsored by one of the largest corporations located in Saint Louis. I can't name the company because of a non-disclosure agreement I signed, but I will talk about this experience and the reality of corporate employment in the next chapter.

Takeaways

If you're ever on tech twitter or go to meetups with developers you will frequently hear them lament about how hiring is broken. Initiatives like LaunchCode that help place self taught developers are few and far between. As a result there are many talented developers who are never given a chance to shine because companies are afraid of hiring someone without any work experience or a degree.

To make matters worse, the amount of gatekeeping in the industry tends to disproportionately discourage women from applying to jobs. Just today, a friend of mine posted an update about how she saw a junior software consultant position that required 12 years of experience. It's truly ridiculous how little recruiters understand about posting realistic job descriptions. It's been shown in studies that women typically only apply to jobs where they meet 100% of the criteria, and most men will apply if they meet roughy 60%.

Even if women and other marginalized folks in tech do decide to apply, there is a decent chance they won't be invited to an interview. There was one place in particular where the hiring manager seemed concerned that I was a woman, and he asked me several questions about how comfortable I felt in an "all male" environment. It made me suspect that other women may have been passed up, especially ones that were older than me.

Older women and women of color have it the worst, because they are even smaller minorities in the tech workplace than young white women. At one point my mother was considering enrolling in a bootcamp for data science and I was not sure whether to advise her to do so or not, because I knew how ageism also impacted hiring. My own project manager who is in generation Z lamented to me on several occasions how everyone assumes she is a junior developer but she has actually been in the industry for three decades.

I was lucky that I had the means to move to Saint Louis and the ability to lean on my in laws for financial support. For people living in major cities like New York or DC, it's much more difficult to get your foot in the door. Employers in these cities can pick and choose from hundreds of candidates, so even if you have been teaching yourself to code for two years and have a stellar portfolio you can still be passed up just because you don't have any previous work experience.

I really don't know what I would have done without Launch-Code. They had all of the connections to the local community that I didn't have, and organizations were motivated to hire from them because of the bonus feel-good aspect and the fact that LaunchCode would then be sure to improve their reputation in the city.

LaunchCode has also done a great job of attracting more tech companies to the Saint Louis area. Stripe, the ubiquitous card reader that attaches to your phone or tablet, has a major hub there now. There is also a great accelerator downtown in a building known as T-Rex where many startups have gotten space to grow and build something valuable.

The only downside to organizations like LaunchCode is that sometimes people starting out get the wrong idea about the hype around coding. Maybe one of those elitist engineers I mentioned in earlier chapters told them that learning to code is easy, that it's the best option for them, and that with the added training from LaunchCode they will pick it up in no time. Sadly there are some people who drop out when they realize this isn't the case. Some of them even become bitter towards the organization for what they believe to be false advertising.

Despite the criticism from the jaded, I still think LaunchCode has done a lot to benefit the community. While there are tons of resources online, nothing replaces having a mentor in person walking you through the code. For LaunchCode to provide those types of resources for free is really special.

9

The Would-Be Hackathon

Memories

I wish I could say the first company I was placed at by LaunchCode was a success. I already had a few interviews at various startups but never received a call back and things were looking a bit grim. That was when Kelly called me about a different kind of opportunity. A large company in Saint Louis was staging a hackathon and they wanted LaunchCode to pick out their "best and brightest" candidates to participate.

Though I cannot disclose a lot of details around the hackathon project itself because of an ironclad NDA, I will do my best to describe overall what the experience was like. Honestly the technical stack itself is mostly irrelevant because what I learned from this hackathon was really about corporate culture and how to distinguish the real from the fake.

The reason I agreed to the hackathon in the first place was because of the hype surrounding the project. It was described to me as a golden opportunity to be on the front lines of creating a new special unit within the corporation that would operate like a startup but without the added risks and lack of funds that a startup typically has to worry about. I had heard of this trend before around companies like Capital One that were eager to keep pace with their smaller but more nimble competitors.

This all sounded well and good, but there was one catch: our hackathon team would have to deliver the application in just a few weeks in order to convince the executives. At this point I should have already sensed some of the red flags; if it was up to the executives to decide whether this special unit was going to be made, what guarantee could the hackathon leader really promise us? How much did the executives even know about what was going on? What exactly were the standards that we were being measured against? The answer to pretty much all of the above questions turned out to be: nothing.

I still remember the anxiety I felt when I came into the first meeting with my new teammates. The hackathon organizers had really hyped it up and made me feel like I was someone that would be delivering the moon and the stars. As a result I felt extremely nervous about my ability to build the product. I could sense the nervousness of my teammates sitting next to me as well. In fact, one of the guys dropped out of the project after that initial meeting. Perhaps he saw the writing on the wall before I did, or perhaps he was just too intimidated. I will never know.

At the time I had zero experience with corporate lingo or any of the bravado that comes along with belonging to a prominent organization. Very little concrete information was given to us in the first meeting, and when we started to actually discuss the technical requirements of the project it became pretty clear that we needed access to a slew of company resources in order to build what they wanted. It would have been fine if we could just make a mock up, but they insisted that the app could not be considered complete until it had real data.

A week flew by in no time. Then another week. We still had not been given access to the data we needed to execute the project. I had built some mockups and powerpoint presentations to explain what we were doing to stakeholders. My teammates were doing what they could with dummy data. All in all the hackathon was shaping up to be something more like an endurance race. It wasn't clear when or even if we were going to get the resources we needed to complete the project. A lot of the initial enthusiasm of our lead seemed to wearing off too.

Every way we turned we met resistance. It was almost like the organizer of the hackathon had no idea what would be necessary to accomplish the project when he proposed it. Hardly anyone we talked to seemed to be in the loop on what we were doing, and the ones who were seemed very dubious about it. One of the employees at the company even went so far as to say we had probably been conned all in the name of someone hoping to get a raise for initiating this pet project.

By this point I had made friends with most of the guys on the team, though one in particular was nice enough to give me a ride from the company headquarters because he lived near me. He was down to earth and also suspicious of what was going on, but the way he saw it when there was nothing to do he could spend time learning the skills he really wanted to learn and get paid for it, so he was willing to put up with the arrangement despite the frustration.

About a month in another one of our teammates decided he was going to leave. Our day to day life had become sitting in a dreary office occasionally harassing some of the employees about the status of the resources we needed and hoping they would respond. I couldn't really blame him, as I was back on the phone with LaunchCode myself and letting them know I was probably going to be looking at other opportunities.

It took about three months before the project finally began wrapping up, and there was not even a whisper about anymore fast paced special unit being created within the company. In fact, the entire demeanor of the hackathon organizer had morphed into someone completely different. I still wonder what the man had been hoping to accomplish, or if he had actually fooled himself as much as he had been fooling us. At the end of it all the company actually tried to convince me to stay on as a powerpoint designer. Naturally, I declined.

When I got on the phone with my LaunchCode recruiter to tell her what happened, she did not seem surprised. It turned out that this wasn't the first time that this particular company had misled LaunchCode about their intentions. She told me everyone they had placed there was not very satisfied with their position, and that I would probably be better off somewhere else. As disappointed as I felt going back to square one, I knew there was no way I would be going in the direction I wanted if I was designing powerpoints for a living. A very far cry from my expectations. It seemed that the best option was to take my chances with another company.

Takeaways

As I mentioned in the last section, this was my first real experience with corporate culture. I had no idea the amount of bullshitting and ass kissing that took place in those environments. Granted, those problems existed in academia too, but the nature of corporate bullshitting was different enough that it still threw me for a loop.

I thought that because it was harder to prove the value you were providing in an academic setting, bureaucratic bloat would be more common there. My idea of corporations was that they had little tolerance for clunky processes and expected everything to be delivered quickly and precisely. This notion was completely and utterly shattered by my experience with this corporation.

The reason I wanted to include this weird three month experience was because I ended up having similar problems in other companies I worked at later on. It wouldn't be the last time that the job description ended up being dramatically different from reality. Tech companies are not above luring prospective employees into positions with promises they can't keep. Those promises could be about the technical stack you are using, or about the project management standards they keep, or even about things like health insurance or time off (though that is less common).

Sometimes the lures are intentionally set, and sometimes the recruiter or hiring manager simply doesn't know what they are talking about and gives you the wrong information. Either way, at the end of the day it will be you who suffers the most from buying into it. If you know someone inside the company, make sure you reach out to them. Usually if something sounds outrageous, it's because it probably is and someone in the organization had the wrong idea.

A friend of mine had something like this happen to her. Basically, a recruiter reached out to her about a senior position in a company she had applied to previously. Even though she was okay with her current role she decided the company was interesting enough and it might be worth the jump. After doing an IQ test followed by a remote and in person technical assessment, she was told that she was not qualified enough for a senior position. In fact, they didn't even think she was qualified for a mid-level position. The recruiter told her they could only hire her as as intern!

Naturally this outraged my friend (who had four years of programming experience) greatly, and I spent an evening listening to her rant about it. Everyone told her that this was insulting, and she should move on. For a week it looked like that's what she was going to do, but then the director of engineering gave her a phone call. Apparently the recruiter was new to the company, and had misunderstood the hiring managers decision. They did want to hire her as a mid level engineer, and just wanted to give her one final assessment that was originally designed for the interns: hence the source of confusion.

That is just one outrageous example, but there are many others, and not all of them have the same outcome. Sometimes the outrageous incident is intentional and a product of toxic company culture. For instance, I had an experience interviewing for a government contracting position a few years ago where there were a lot of red flags. Namely, the fact that they kept interviewing me and failing to come to a decision. I think by the end of the process I had gone through six or seven interviews. Even some of the people who interviewed me admitted that it was getting ridiculous, but they couldn't seem to come up to a decision.

Unfortunately I took that job despite the rocky interview experience, and ended up regretting it deeply later on. I only lasted there six months before the disorganization and hectic schedule started to drive me insane. To make matters worse, a few months after that a number of my friends who worked there were laid off because the company lost a major client. I ended up making the jump just in the nick of time.

With all of the numerous ways a job can go wrong, what is an entry level programmer supposed to do? I would argue that there are certain soft skills that are a must to develop. The biggest soft skills of them all is your bullshit detector. If you're one of those lucky people who has always been able to spot a liar, then you might already be in a good place. For the rest of us, the bullshit detector can take months and often years to develop.

Personally, I still fall for bullshit sometimes. I think it might be a skill I will continue to develop for the rest of my life. The hardest part is that bullshit in the tech industry can come in so many forms. It might be your manager promising that you will get to do more backend work after the acquisition. Maybe it's your coworker insisting that his teammates in the office take your code reviews seriously. It could be the principal engineer interrupting you in every front end meeting because he thinks his ideas are better even though he hasn't touched a CSS document in his entire life.

Here I will offer my best suggestions for spotting the bullshit early on, which will hopefully help you avoid some of the pain I've experienced over the years. If you're a generally nervous person during interviews, consider recording the interview and listening back to it later. This works best for phone calls. I have learned that when I am nervous I am too focused on preparing what I will say to pay attention to red flags from the person interviewing me.

Another way to gauge how good a company is when you are deciding whether to accept an offer or not is by looking at the Glassdoor reviews. While you do end up with some bias in the reviews (usually the most extremely opinionated people are the ones who leave feedback) you can still look at the ratio between positive and negative. If there are a ton of negative reviews and only a few positive ones, chances are that it's not a great place to work. That being said, also pay attention to the dates: companies can change over the years, and just because there were negative reviews in the past doesn't mean the company is awful in the present.

Finally, you should always make friends with people in the tech industry. When you are job hunting, make sure you tell them about your interview experiences. Show them the Glassdoor reviews for the company. Talk to them before your interviews too; they might suggest questions you could ask that you might not have thought of otherwise.

Of course, too many cooks in the kitchen can also ruin the food. If you're feeling decision paralysis it's probably because you've asked too many people for their opinions and naturally, people sometimes disagree. At the end of the day I always suggest that you go with your gut feeling. Even if your internal bullshit detector isn't perfect, your gut can help you make the right decision when your friends might just confuse you and make it impossible to figure out what you should do.

10

The Job Offer

Memories

I can't remember exactly how much time passed between my leaving the hackathon organizing corporation and the time I got my interview with Label Insight, the company that finally made me a job offer as an honest to god Software Engineer. One thing I will never forget is that my very first interview with them was when I was in Italy with my parents. I remember the time difference meant I was doing the interview around 6 or 7PM. I certainly never imagined to be doing an interview on vacation, but it sounded like a cool company and I didn't see any reason to wait.

LabelInsight was focused on making food labels more transparent for consumers by providing a QR code on products that one could scan with their phone. The scan would pull up data that was much more detailed and easier to understand than anything on your standard container. Specific allergens, human readable ingredient definitions, and clear division between claims (healthy cereal) and facts (organic grains).

Frank, the project manager who talked to me in that first video call, is still my friend now. Our conversation was very casual and friendly, and his demeanor put me at ease immediately. He seemed like the kind of person I could work with without a hitch. By the time we finished the interview I felt very good about working at Label Insight. He didn't throw me any curveballs or ask me what I wanted to be doing in 10 years. It was practical and to the point.

My memory about the other interviews is a little bit hazier, but I believe I had the coding test next. It was a javascript coding test that was assigned to me over a special online platform that timed you so you had to finish writing your code within an hour. I liked this approach better than the whiteboard test, because it felt more natural. That being said, I was still nervous about the timed aspect.

These days there are hundreds of different online testing platforms to choose from, but I was lucky that the one Label Insight chose did not assign extremely challenging questions. I did my best to focus on the question at hand and not worry too much about the time limit, except for when I was clearly not making any headway and needed to try a different approach. It also helped that I did some preparation questions in advance. Sometimes those types of online tests take you back to college algorithms, and it's always worth it to brush up on them.

As you probably guessed, I passed the coding test without a hitch. In fact I was surprised to learn that I passed the test in the top 90th percentile. There was definitely a stupid grin on my face when the principal engineer gave me that news in my following phone call. My memory of that conversation is far more foggy, but I know the fact that I did not have any

AngularJS experience must have come up at some point. It was a relief when they told me they were confident based on my score results that I could learn AngularJS on the job.

The last and final stage was an in person interview where I got to see the company office, meet the team, and resolve any final questions or concerns I might have. Frankly, I was so thrilled to get this far in the process, questions and concerns were not very high on my list. I had an interview with one other company that I was waiting to hear back from, but it was a consulting firm that I already had some reservations about. Label Insight was my best chance, so I was focused on making a good impression.

I wish I could recall more details from the in person interview. I remember getting a bit of a mixed vibe from the developers when I introduced myself, because they were all very focused on their work and only briefly shook my hand. Later on I ended up making friends with most of them, so clearly my initial impression was misplaced. Sometimes you can't put too much weight on introductions.

I also had a short meeting with the CTO, where he asked me how I felt about the company as a whole and how I imagined myself within it. I told him I could picture myself working there pretty easily, and that I appreciated the laid back atmosphere and the chance to learn a popular Javascript framework. That apparently sealed the deal, because the CTO gave me the offer letter then and there. It was a surreal moment for sure, and I remember staring dumbly at the piece of paper like I couldn't believe he was actually giving it to me.

That was it. Right there in front of me was the validation I had been working towards since college. I could not believe these people who I had only met a few weeks ago actually believed

I had what it took to be a software engineer. It sounded so much fancier than anything I had imagined. Maybe front end developer, or web developer, or even something more generic than that. But surely I didn't deserve the title of software engineer.

Despite all my doubts the paper in front of me did not lie. It was a real job offer, one that I could hold and feel with my shaking hands. I stopped in a coffee shop on the way home and called my parents to tell them the good news. It felt so good to be able to tell my family that I had made it, that all of those risks I took were not for nothing. I talked to my dad for almost an hour before I realized how much time had gone by. Truly I was giddy with excitement.

The next day I signed the offer letter. It marks the beginning of a new chapter in my career, where I began to work my way up the engineering hierarchy, and even begin to pass on some of my knowledge and experience like I tried to do in these pages. Hopefully having read this book you will feel better prepared as you venture forth to try and land that first job. It won't be easy, but it will be worth it.

Takeaways

This is it. The final section of this book. It doesn't have as many anecdotes or detailed examples as I would like, because a lot of years have gone by and I feel disingenuous filling in the gaps with dramatized versions of the truth. That being said, I did my best to impart everything I learned from getting my foot in the door. There was a lot of trial and error that I hope you will be in a better position to learn from now.

Because some years have gone by, I am sure not all of

experience will apply to you. There are more resources to learn from now than when I was starting out. AngularJS is outdated now and you have new frameworks like Vue and React. The tech industry moves fast and its really hard to keep up, so I tried to keep this book focused on the tactics I used to feel my way rather than specific tools that might not be relevant anymore.

When you finally get that offer, it might feel as surreal to you as it did to me. If you live in a big city where engineers are plentiful, you may have to apply to a lot more jobs and receive a lot more rejections than I did before that glorious day. Certainly, since I started out, a lot more bootcamps have cropped up over the country that have changed the landscape of hiring for developers.

If I had the time and energy I would write about all the jobs I had after I got my foot in the door. Maybe in a few more years there will be a book on that subject. However, those first few years struggling without the help or validation from coworkers are the hardest. Keeping up the motivation to learn something as overwhelming and dense as how to code can drain all the energy out of you. If you can get past that, all of the struggles in the workplace will seem pretty tame in comparison.

It's even worse if you are a minority and tech struggling to find role models and mentors who know what it's like to suffer from imposter syndrome. There were very few women in tech for me to look up to as I was making this journey. The vast majority were men who told me that coding was easy and struggled to explain things in a way that made sense to me. Thats why figuring out how you learn best is so crucial.

I want to end this book with a story from Ashley, a friend of mine who transitioned from working in physical therapy to being a developer in her 30's. She was burning out fast at her day job, faster than she could learn to code. For several years before things got too stressful Ashely would do simple web development freelance work here and there. As the burnout got worse, she decided she needed to learn Javascript and had to set aside more time.

Eventually she was so stressed out that she changed her physical therapist schedule to just work on weekends. At that point she was pretty well practiced in her field, so the pay was good and she was able to afford working fewer hours. This freed up her weekdays to build her coding portfolio while continuing to learn javascript.

A friend of Ashley's then got her a recruiter who placed her in her first tech job. Unfortunately, it left much to be desired. Turned out that it was primarily data entry, but for a huge site redesign. Since the pay was poor, she was still working part time as a physical therapist, and still not getting the experience she really wanted. This was a really low point for her, where desperation started to set in. Ashley admitted that she felt like a failure for spending money on graduate school and ending up in a career she was not happy with.

Luckily that period did not last long, because the data entry she was doing was for a big name company. Having that company's name on her resume ended up being a significant boon. She was able to get a new role a few months later where she had access to other developers who could train her up and help her move from content production to actual development work. In her own words, Ashley said she had to be very annoying to make any progress in her tech career. If she didn't ask lots of questions and insist on getting the developers attention, she thinks she might still be doing data entry even now.

I wanted to leave you with that story because your own background will obviously change your experience getting into tech dramatically. Ashley had a much more trying time than I did working her way up to becoming a developer. However, she still had the determination, motivation, and patience to pull it off. It's so important to advocate for yourself during the process, and not let other people put you down. Sometimes that means being annoying and asking questions even when part of you just wants to stay quiet. Sometimes it means taking a break even when you think one more try will solve the problem.

Ashley is a lot happier now, with a little boy and a comfortable job working remotely while being a mom. Working in tech is not perfect, but it lends a lot of comfort and freedom to a persons life that not many other careers offer. Certainly it has its stressful moments and not all tech jobs are equal. If you work at Facebook or Amazon you will have a very different perspective from someone working for Oracle. But unlike most industries, technical skills are in such high demand that there are opportunities in almost every city in the country and abroad.

That is not a call for every person in the country to learn to code, but if you are already interested I think there is very little reason not to give it a shot. Believe in yourself, watch out for the pitfalls, and be patient with yourself as you progress. While it won't happen overnight, if you can stick with it you will find rewards on the other side. Maybe five years from now you will build a money making web application and start your own business. Maybe you will be the first female engineer in your company. Maybe you will even write a book about your tech journey. There's only one way to find out!

Author Note

Thank you so much for reading my book. I started writing it in July of 2018 and honestly almost gave up after writing the first 7,000 words. Initially my thinking was to write a much longer book that also detailed my experiences at the various companies I worked at, both large and small. What I quickly realized though was that this task was going to make the book a lot more difficult to organize. As someone who has always worked most effectively in sprints, I should have known that aiming to cover that much ground was probably not very realistic. Maybe when I retire I will write that type of book, when I don't have to fear any repercussions on my career.

In September of 2019, after over a year of not touching the book, I started a new job and felt a burst of confidence. What really brought it together was joining a community called Women Make, which was running a challenge to ship a product in one month. I looked at some of the projects that had been completed the previous year, and some of them were ebooks that were relatively short, about 20,000 words. Remembering that I had already written 7,500 words of my book a year ago, I realized that maybe I could limit the scope and actually ship a shorter book before the holiday season.

Knowing I had a tight deadline and running on the high of landing a cool new job, I was able to fuel my writing during the month of October. I decided I could write a book for people starting in tech who couldn't afford a bootcamp or an expensive education and wanted to teach themselves. After all, this was my own journey, and it was incredibly difficult on my own. At times I really thought that I was never going to accomplish anything, and that I was risking it all by moving to Saint Louis without any job lined up. Some of my friends genuinely thought I was crazy, and I feared they were right.

If you found this book helpful, inspiring, or that it at least made you feel a little less alone while making your way in tech, I could not emphasize enough how much a review would mean to me. I have read every review my readers have left on Amazon, and always take the feedback seriously. If there is something my book could have done better, I want to hear about it. Likewise it always warms my heart when something I wrote has made a positive difference in someone's life. If you would like to leave a review now, please follow this link.

About the Author

Nadya Primak is a self-taught software engineer with a bachelors degree in Visual Arts and Russian from Oberlin College. She has four years of experience working in the tech industry at companies both large and small. Nadya is also an indie game developer and has published several games including Nightcrawler VR Bowling and Grand Canyon Adventure among others. Of course a good game developer should also play games, and Nadya spends a fair amount of her free time doing just that with her husband. When she doesn't have a controller in her hand she is probably watching a psychological thriller, drawing on her tablet, or looking at cat pictures on Instagram.

You can connect with me on:
- http://nadyaprimak.com
- https://twitter.com/nadyaprimak
- https://bit.ly/3fOdlao

Subscribe to my newsletter:
✉ https://mailchi.mp/712638547bc6/subscribe

www.ingramcontent.com/pod-product-compliance
Lightning Source LLC
Chambersburg PA
CBHW021500210526
45463CB00002B/827